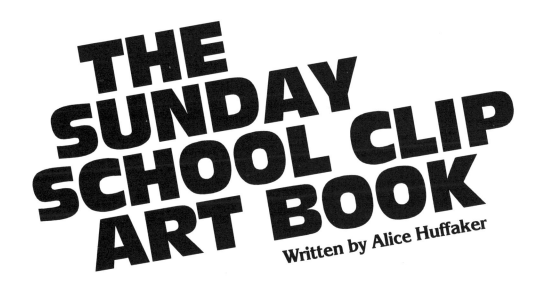

THE SUNDAY SCHOOL CLIP ART BOOK

Written by Alice Huffaker

Featuring the art of Chizuko Yasuda,
Rick Bundschuh, Chris Wilson, Tom Finley,
Joyce Thimsen and Barbara LeVan

THE SUNDAY SCHOOL CLIP ART BOOK

3 4 5 6 7 8 9 / 91 90 89 88

CONTENTS

MAILERS IN TEN EASY STEPS

HERE'S HOW YOU DO IT!

Follow the simple, step-by-step instructions given here and you will produce appealing, eye-catching printed pieces.

PART ONE: THE TOOLS AND SUPPLIES YOU NEED

You can buy these tools and supplies at art supply stores, stationery stores and many department stores.

- Scratch pad and pen for writing the rough draught
- White cardstock, cardboard or paper
- A pencil and pencil sharpener
- An eraser (even the pros make an occasional mistake)
- Rubber cement
- Paper towels to clean up excess rubber cement
- A ruler (preferably 18-inch flexible steel)
- A 45° triangle, to help lay out guidelines. A clear plastic triangle allows you to see through it as you draw lines.
- Three black felt pens (fine, medium, and wide point) for hand lettering
- Liquid Paper brand correction fluid (for correcting mistakes you can't erase)
- Scissors
- And, of course, this book.

Optional Tools and Materials:
- An X-Acto knife or equivalent. Buy #11 blades which are shaped like this:

The most comfortable knife to work with is shaped like a fountain pen.

- Speedball brand nibs and handles. They make cleaner letters than felt pens. We recommend that you get Speedball nibs B-6 (fine line), B-5 ½, B-5 (mediums) and one or two wide nibs for writing headlines. Buy a handle for each nib.

- Ink for the pens. Black Magic brand ink (don't worry, it's not demonic!) is probably the best. If you will be using much ink, buy a large refill bottle. It's cheaper that way.

- A compass for drawing circles.

- An electric pencil sharpener or manual pencil pointer.

- Technical pens. Technical drawing pens are expensive little toys which require constant cleaning. However, they can be very useful. Ask at your art store for Mars, Rapid-O-Graph and other brands.

- A drawing table and drawing lamp.

- Graph paper lined with light blue ink. The lines will help you keep your art and lettering straight and the light blue lines don't reproduce on photocopiers or printing presses.

A Helpful Suggestion:

There are thousands of different transfer (rub-on or peel-and-stick) alphabets, numbers and backgrounds (dots, stripes, etc.) available in large sheets. Here are some examples:

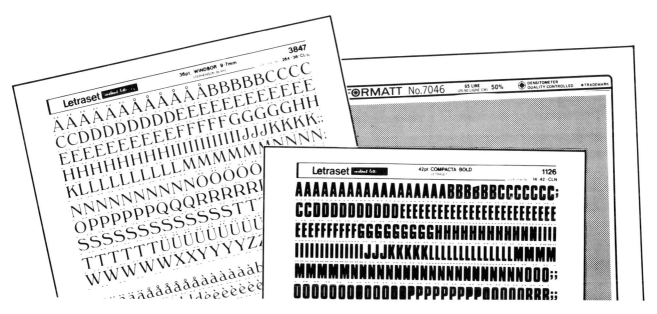

Ask at your art store to see the manufacturers' catalogs. You can choose just the right letters or backgrounds to give your printed pieces that extra little bit of appeal. Although rub-on and peel-and-stick letters take a long time to apply, they give your material a professional look.

Store sheets in plastic envelopes to keep the letters and art from chipping and cracking.

PART TWO: THE TECHNIQUE

Here's the simple way to turn a blank sheet of paper into a masterpiece.

The basic formula:

| Blank paper | Clip art from this book | Scissors, rubber cement, etc. | Your own handwriting or typing. Optional: Transfer (rub-on) letters and art. |

An appealing work of art and literature!

Now, let's make a mail out . . .

STEP ONE: Decide what your mailer will be about. Write a rough draft.

STEP TWO: Decide what the format of your mailer will be. Will it be on 8 ½ × 11-inch paper? Or, will it be 11 × 17-inches? Or, will you make it an odd size which will require trimming from a standard size when it is printed? Some small print shops can't handle 11 × 17-inch paper, so check ahead.

STEP THREE: Cut a "paste-up sheet" the same size as the final product. This is the sheet on which you will rubber cement the artwork, draw the lettering, and write or type your message. Then you will deliver your paste-up sheet to the printer. Always handle the paste-up sheet with care so that you don't smudge it or get fingerprints on it. We suggest that your paste-up sheet be cut from heavy cardstock. Cardstock is easy to cut to size and more durable than paper. You may also use graph paper lined with light blue lines. Buy high quality graph paper so that the ink you use will not bleed and turn fuzzy.

STEP FOUR: Find the appropriate pieces of artwork in this book. For example:

Cut the artwork out of the book. Each page is perforated for easy removal. Most of the artwork has been reproduced in more than one size to give you flexibility in page design.

STEP FIVE: Decide where to position the art and your copy. Either make a few pencil sketches on scratch paper or decide in your mind the basic arrangement you will use. Plan to leave a one-half inch (or more) margin on your paper, unless you plan to "bleed" your art (see glossary in the "How to Survive the Printers" section of this book).

STEP SIX: Use rubber cement, following the manufacturer's directions, to glue the artwork to the paste-up sheet. Rubber cement is not permanent, so handle your paste-up sheet gently. We recommend rubber cement because it is easy to use and clean up.

STEP SEVEN: Use a pencil and triangle to draw straight guidelines for lettering. Or, use graph paper.

STEP EIGHT: Letter on white paper headlines or other copy that will not be typewritten. Use black felt pens, pen and ink or transfer letters. Follow the manufacturer's instruction when using transfer letters.

A HELPFUL REMINDER: Avoid the frustration of ruining your paste-up with lettering mistakes by lettering on a separate sheet of paper. Cut out your lettering and rubber cement it to your paste-up sheet.

STEP NINE: After the paste-up is dry, correct all errors and erase all pencil lines. There you have it—a wonderful mailer.

STEP TEN: Now you are ready to take your mail-out to the print shop. Turn to the "HOW TO SURVIVE THE PRINTERS" section of this book for tips about how to get your mailer printed. Or, if you intend to photocopy your mailer, read "TIPS ON PHOTOCOPYING."

BABIES AND YOUNG CHILDREN

Welcome to our Nursery

Welcome to our Nursery

16

CHOMP!

CHOMP!

PLEASE FEED YOUR CHILDREN
BEFORE CLASS

PLEASE FEED YOUR CHILDREN
BEFORE CLASS

WHILE
PUSHING
DOWN
TURN
TO OPEN

CHILDREN

25

26

FAMILIES

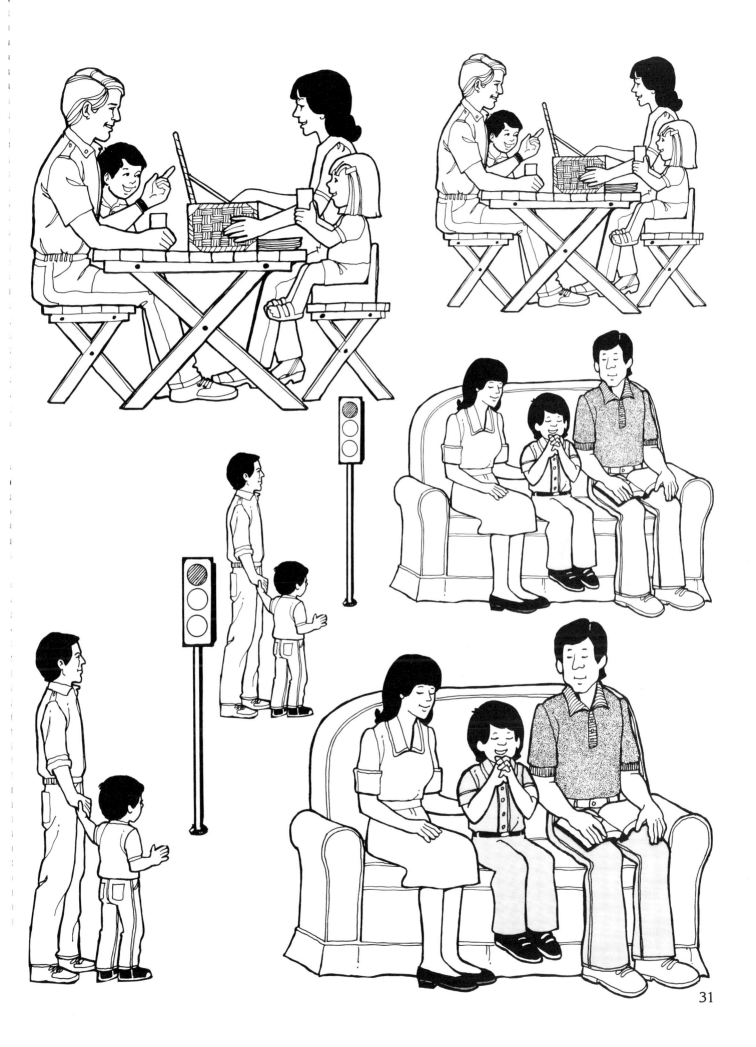

BIBLE PEOPLE

35

ANIMALS

PATTERNS

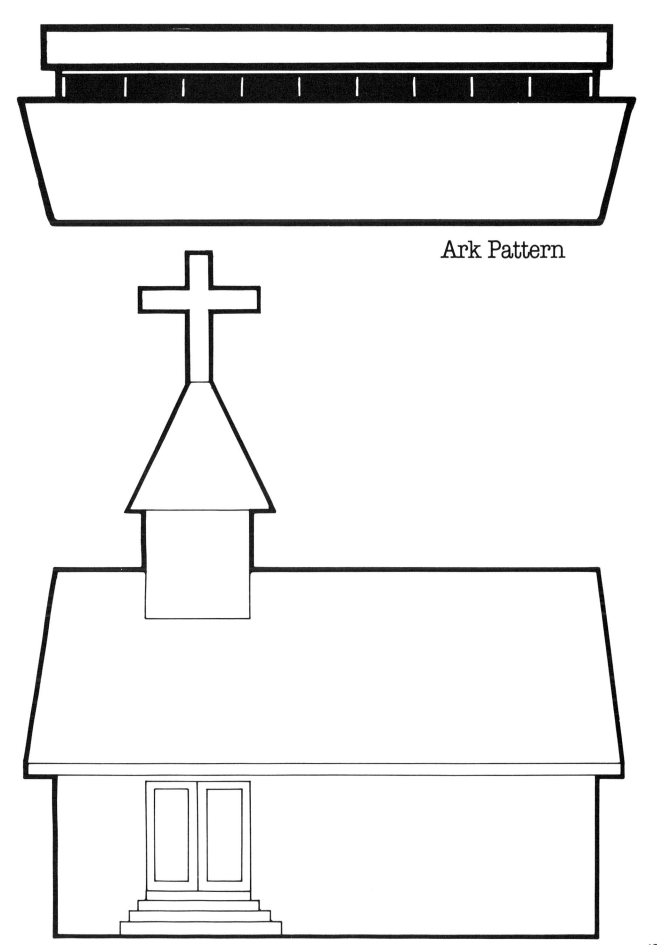

Ark Pattern

42

Finger puppet

43

45

Write a message on the flower petals. When your teachers or children put the flower together, they'll get your message.

Palm Branch Pattern

46

Blanket

Water bag

Finger puppet

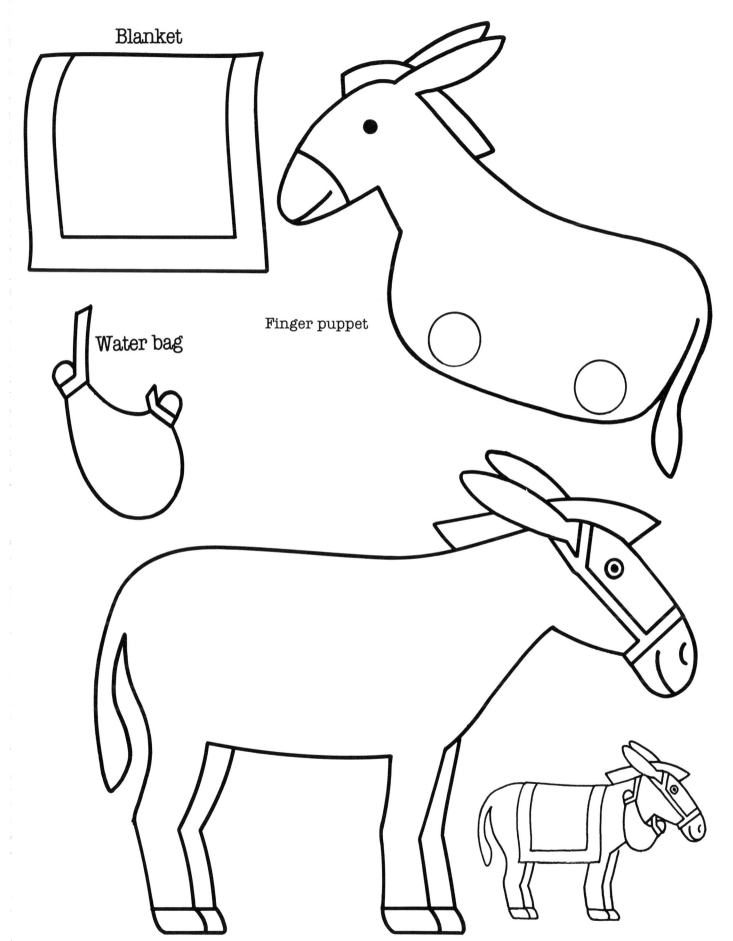

(child's name)

49

50

51

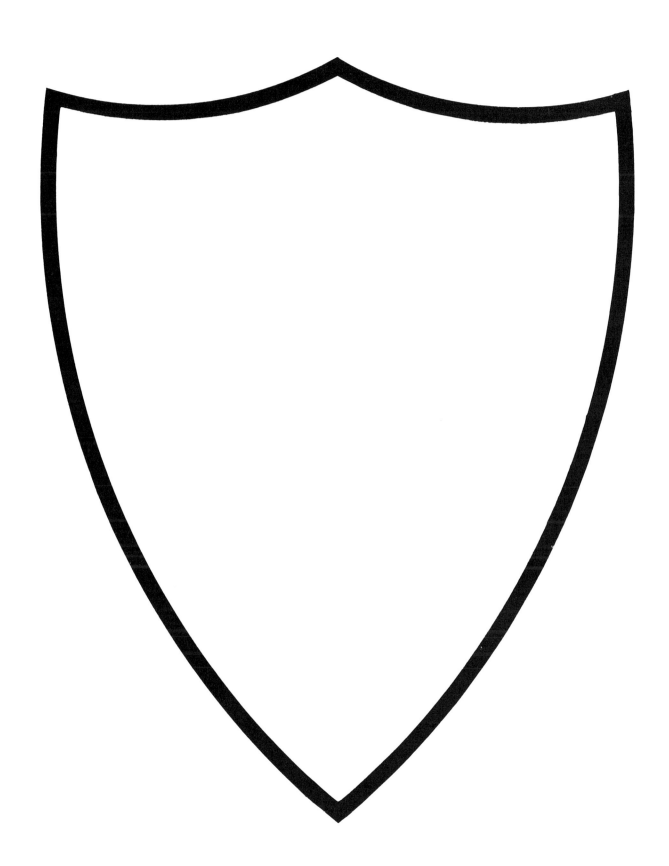

52

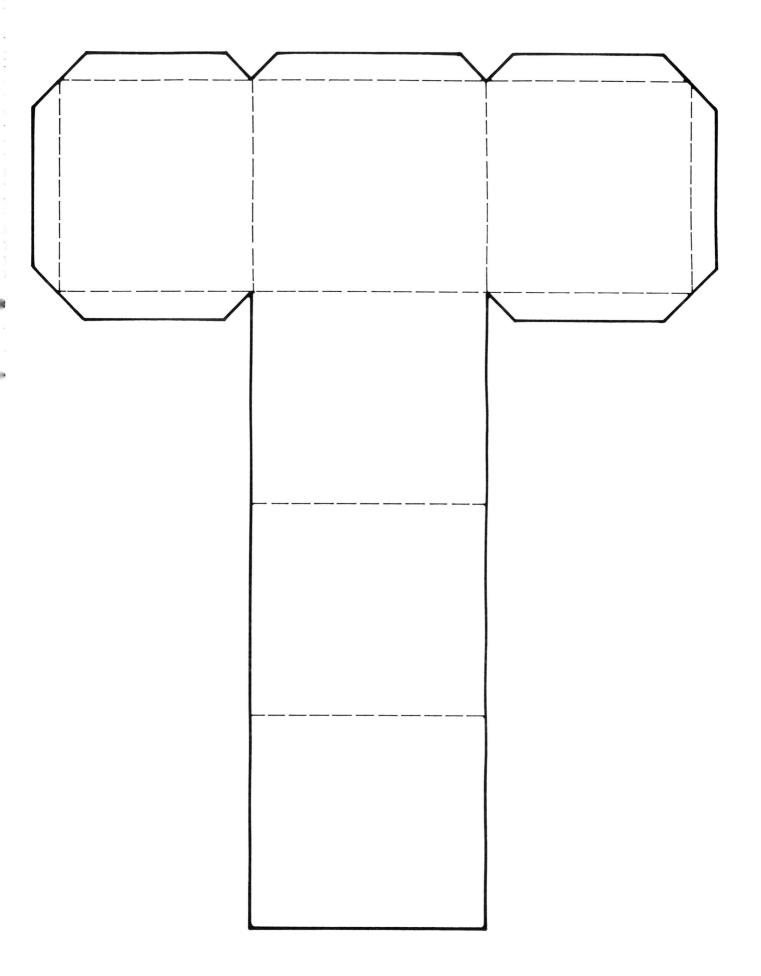

54

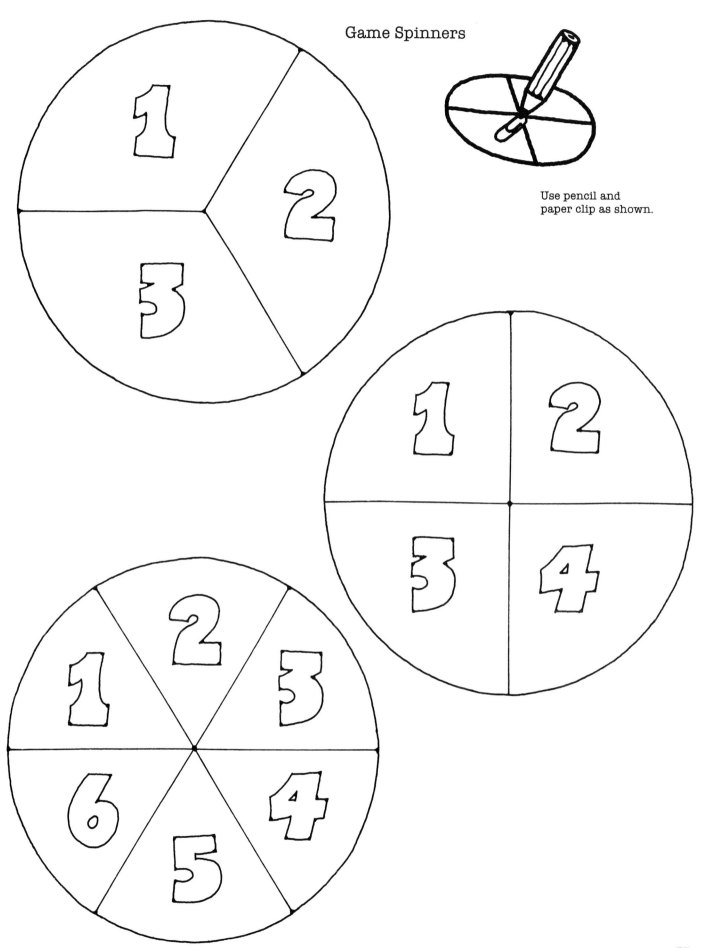

Game Spinners

Use pencil and
paper clip as shown.

55

SPECIAL EVENTS

C'mon! It's Time for VBS

59

SEASONS

63

64

66

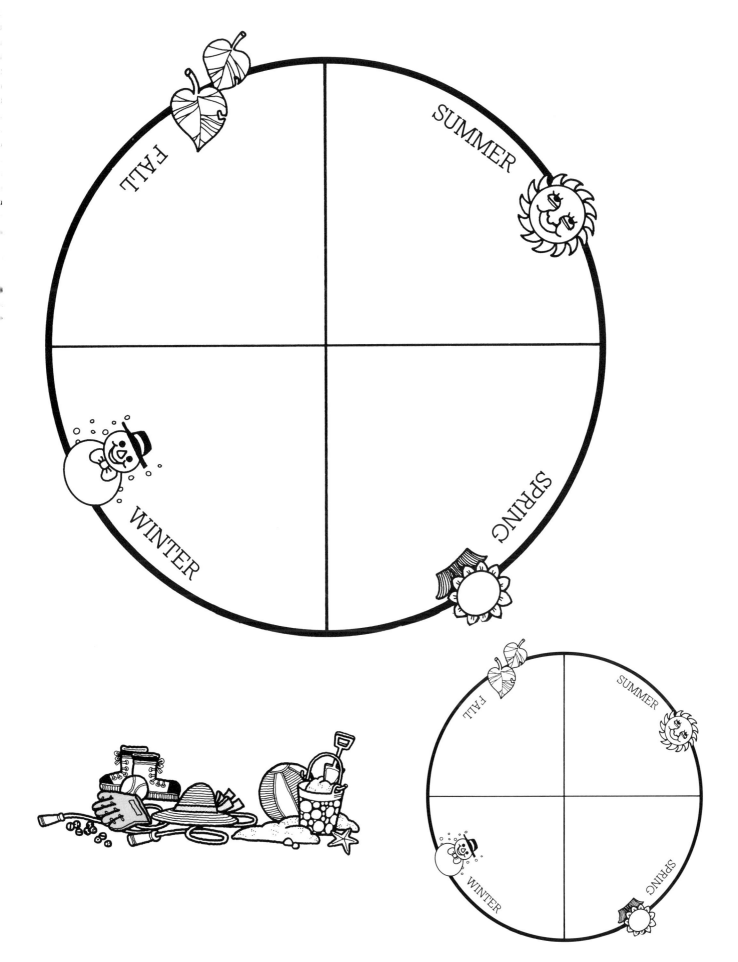

BORDERS

NOTES

NOTES

NOTES

NOTES

73

74

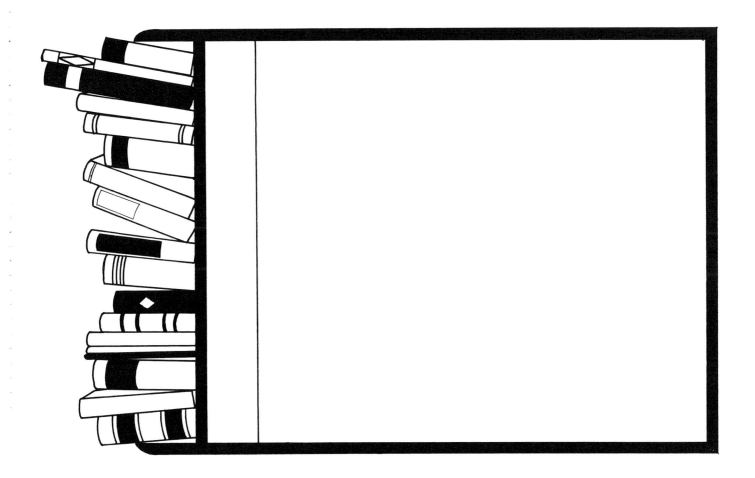

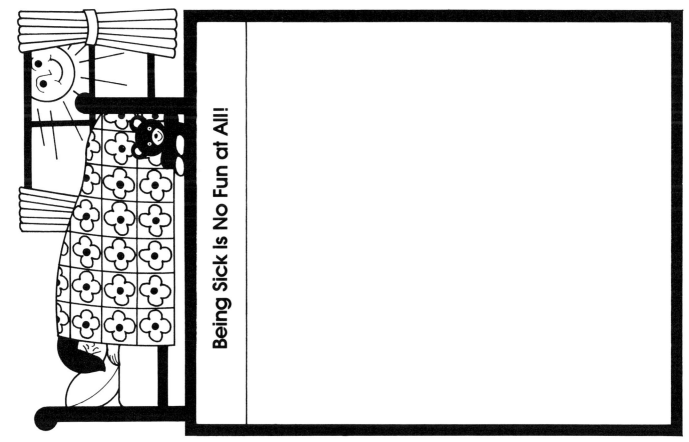

Being Sick Is No Fun at All!

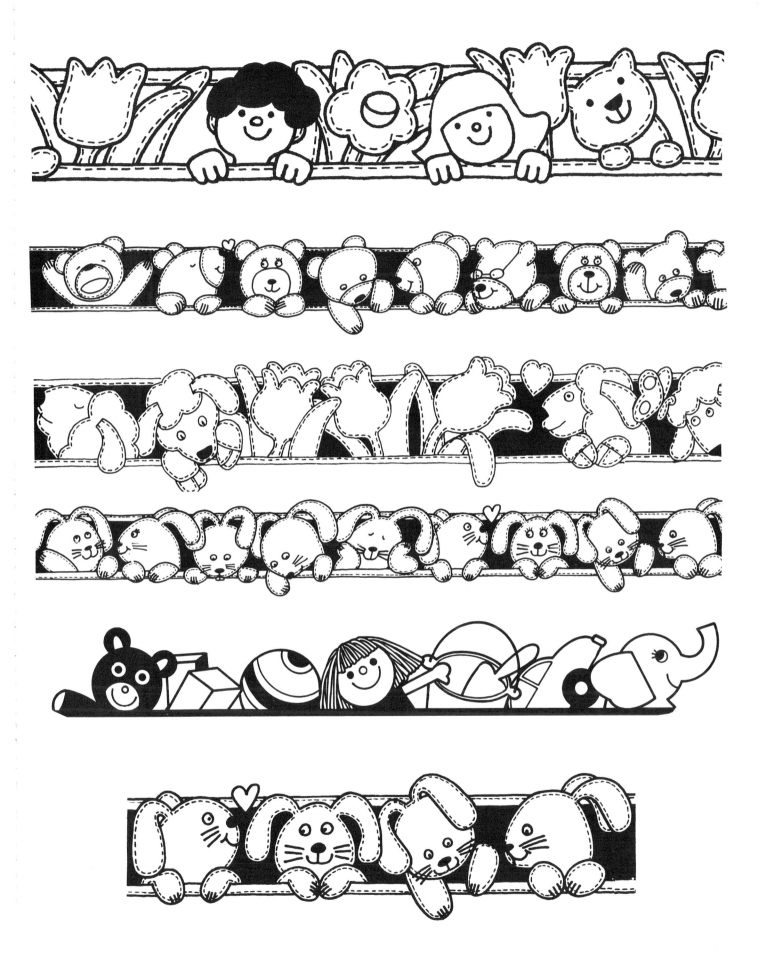

Jesus loves you.

CARDS AND AWARDS

The Lord will watch over your coming and going – now and always *See Psalm 121:8*

The Lord will watch over your coming and going – now and always *See Psalm 121:8*

It's Fun to go to Church

It's Fun to go to Church

Blue Ribbon

Blue Ribbon

GOOD
HELPER

GOOD
HELPER

GOOD
HELPER

Are you feeling better?

Are you feeling better?

Are you feeling better?

93

Happy Birthday you are one year old!

Happy Birthday you are two years old!

HEADLINES

Barbeque Barbeque Barbeque

We're going to the beach

We're going to the beach **We're going to the beach**

It's Time for Backyard Bible School

It's Time for Backyard Bible School

It's Time for Backyard Bible School

Bike Hike ***Bike Hike*** ***Bike Hike***

Happy Birthday! *Happy Birthday!*

Happy Birthday!

Campout **Campout** **Campout**

Coming Soon! *Coming Soon!* *Coming Soon!*

Congratulations! *Congratulations!*

Congratulations!

Don't Forget Don't Forget

Don't Forget

Happy Easter! Happy Easter!

Happy Easter!

Fireworks Festival

Fireworks Festival   Fireworks Festival

Games! Games! Games!

Games! Games! Games!   Games! Games! Games!

Hike   Hike   Hike

IMPORTANT   IMPORTANT   IMPORTANT

Important   Important   Important

important   important   important

Let's Get Together

Let's Get Together   Let's Get Together

Mark It on Your Calendar

Mark It on Your Calendar   Mark It on Your Calendar

Merry Christmas

Merry Christmas   Merry Christmas

NEWS NEWS NEWS

News News News

news *news* *news*

Picnic **Picnic** **Picnic**

All Church Picnic All Church Picnic

All Church Picnic

Come to the Picnic Come to the Picnic

Come to the Picnic

We're Having a Picnic

We're Having a Picnic We're Having a Picnic

It's Time for Pizza! **It's Time for Pizza!**

It's Time for Pizza!

Planning Meeting

Planning Meeting **Planning Meeting**

Pool Party **Pool Party** **Pool Party**

Rejoice! **Rejoice!** **Rejoice!**

We're going to the shore

We're going to the shore **We're going to the shore**

Summer Camp
Summer Camp
Summer Camp

Happy Valentines Day

Happy Valentines Day *Happy Valentines Day*

ANNOUNCING—VBS!

ANNOUNCING—VBS! ### ANNOUNCING—VBS!

Wiener Roast
Wiener Roast ### Wiener Roast

Winter Camp
Winter Camp ### Winter Camp

You Are Invited *You Are Invited* *You Are Invited*

Let's Go to the Zoo

Let's Go to the Zoo *Let's Go to the Zoo*

MISCELLANEOUS ART

PARK

PARK

100

101

Thank You, God, for Springtime

For Kittens · Sunshine · God's Love · Flowers

Thank You, God, for Springtime

For Kittens · Sunshine · God's Love · Flowers

104

106

107

110

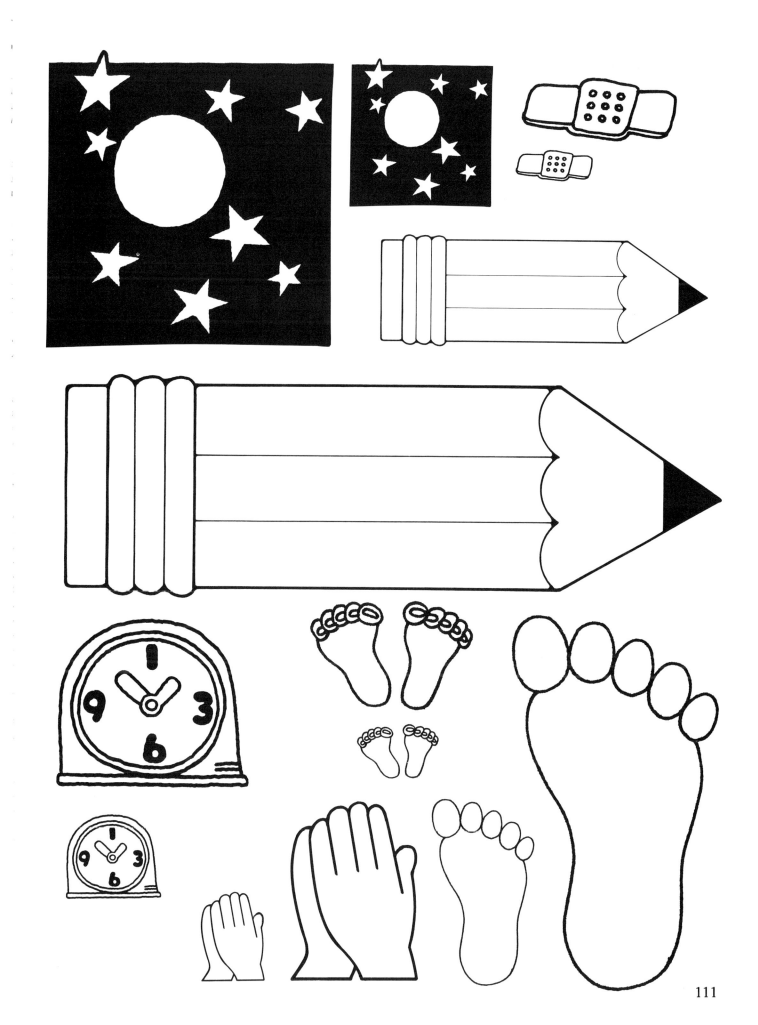

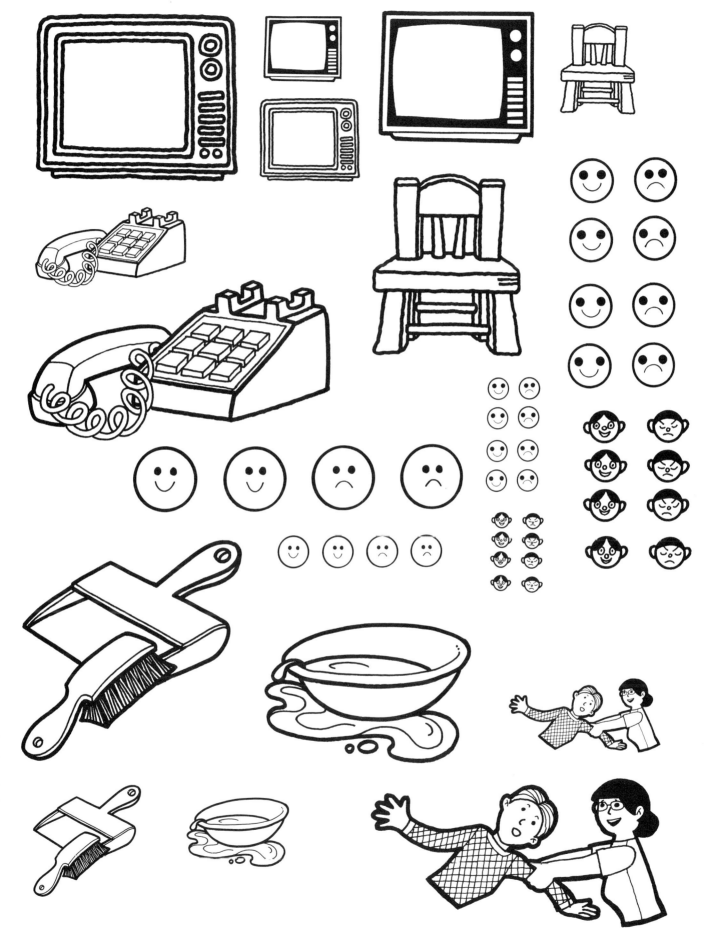

HOW TO SURVIVE THE PRINTERS

Few things are more frustrating than giving a beautiful paste-up job to a printer and then getting it back a few days later printed lopsided and in the wrong color! The following information will help you avoid pitfalls at the printers.

- Shop around by phone for the best deal.

- Ask what kind of paper is available. If you have a large print run (over a few hundred), the printer may need to order paper, which can add days or weeks to the delivery date. Buy the best paper you can afford; it's always worth it.

- The printing press can never, never improve upon what's fed into it. Be sure your paste-up is perfect: all the lines are straight; it's clean; there are no grays (all black); no art is peeling off; every date, fact and figure is correct, and so on.

- Give clear, concise instruction to the printer. Write your instructions on note paper and attach it to the art. Better still, write your instructions on a dummy (see glossary) or a photocopy of your original paste-up.

  Sample instructions:

- Write your name and phone number on the back of the paste-up.

- If you have a second color overlay (see glossary), indicate the color of ink you want to use. (You will be asked to pick the ink from the printer's color samples.) Be sure the printer understands exactly how the overlay is to be aligned with the paste-up sheet.

- Bring money for a deposit.

SERVICES:

All printers provide a list of the services they offer and the cost of each one. Pick up a list. Here is a sample of what you may find on a typical service list:

- Cutting and trimming. The printer can size your printed piece to your specifications. This inexpensive service is well worth the cost. Paying to have your printed pieces trimmed is usually better than trimming the pieces yourself. If much blank paper will be trimmed off and thrown away, why not plan to use it? Design some bookmarks, or write out memory verses to be printed on the blank paper.

- Folding. Printers use fast, accurate folding machines to make large pieces of paper small enough to fit into envelopes. Have you ever tried to tri-fold a thousand mailers by hand?

Bi-fold   **Tri-fold**   **El-foldo**

- Die cuts. A "die" is a handmade tool which will punch any shape you specify into a printed product. The perforations on this page are a type of die cut. Die cutting is expensive, but sometimes you may want to use them. Some Sunday School workers create various shapes of humorous peel and stick labels with a die cut. Another option is to buy a variety of precut labels which are ready to print, peel, and stick.

- Screens. In order to print a photograph, it must be "screened" or broken up into tiny dots. If you are planning to use more than one photo on your printed piece, have the photos reduced to size so that several will fit on the same page. Ask the printer to screen all the photos in one camera shot so that you won't have to pay for screening each individual photograph. Plan to have your photos reduced and screened at the same time—BEFORE you glue them onto your paste-up. Otherwise the printer might mistakenly screen your entire piece of art, breaking up all your fine letters and tiny details into fuzzy little dots.

- Special papers. In addition to the inexpensive bond papers which come in a few standard colors, you can have your artwork printed on heavy cardstock, special finish papers (such as linen or pebble), ultra-bright colors, peel and stick papers, foils (which look like silver or gold leaf) and many other types of paper. Ask your printer for samples.

- Stats. A "stat" is a photographic enlargement or reduction of a piece of art. A printer can stat art to any size you want. You may ask your printer to stat any piece of art in this book—which will come in handy when you are making large posters or tiny stickers.

- Typesetting. Printers do their own typesetting, or they know people who do. If you have a good typesetter in your area, and if you have the piles of silver and gold it takes to hire him or her to typeset your material, you can produce a very nice printed piece. You will probably want to reserve typesetting for a major mailing once a year or so.

GLOSSARY OF ARTIST'S AND PRINTER'S TERMS:

Do you want to sound like you know what you're talking about when you go to the printers? Read over this list.

BLEED: Artwork that extends off the edge of the printed page is said to "bleed." BE SURE your printer has a printing press that can print a bleed if you need one. Many small presses require room at the top of the page to grip the paper. Check with your printer about bleed requirement.

The background bleeds off the printed product.

CAMERA-READY ART: If you have followed the steps given under "MAILERS IN TEN EASY STEPS," then your paste-up sheet should be camera-ready art. That means your art is ready to be made into the plates (see below) which the printer puts on the press. If your original is not camera-ready, your printer will charge you up to $100 an hour to fix it for you. When the printer quotes a price to you, he or she will ask if your art is camera ready—so memorize this one.

CONTINUOUS TONE PHOTOGRAPH: A black and white photo as it comes from a regular camera is called a continuous tone photo: it has shades of gray in it. The photo cannot be printed on a printing press until it has been "screened." See"SCREEN" below.

COPY: All the words, headlines and subheads on your paste-up are referred to collectively as the copy. Body copy is the main section of copy, apart from the headlines.

DUMMY: Hey! Don't get mad! A dummy is a rough draft version of your final art. Write notes to the printer on the dummy.

FLOP: You "flop" an image by photographically making a mirror image like this:

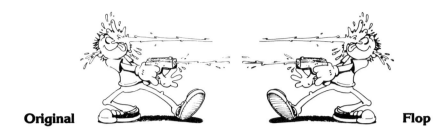

Original   **Flop**

If you want a printer to flop an image, don't use the word "reverse" because that means something entirely different (see below).

FONT: Type comes in thousands of different designs known as "fonts." If you have anything typeset, you will have to pick the various fonts you want. These are examples of several of the most commonly used fonts:

Aa Bb **Cc** **Dd** Ee **Ff**

HALFTONE: A halftone is a photograph that has been "screened." (See "SCREENED" below.)

LINE ART: Art that is pure black and white, with no shades of gray, is called line art. A halftone photograph is really line art. Even the most expensive press can print only solid line art. Look closely at the lithograph hanging on your wall and you will see that each area on it is either a solid color, or fine dots of color. (Incidentally, most full-color reproductions are actually printed in only four colors: black, red, yellow and blue. The tiny dots printed with these colors combine on the page to produce the illusion of full color.)

OVERLAY: A layer of art that is intended to be printed as an additional color on the finished product is called an overlay. Many artists use tissue overlays so they can look through the top layer to the art below it as shown here.

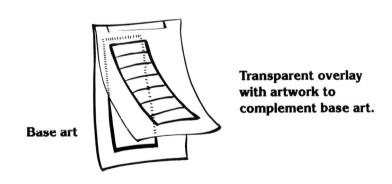

Base art

Transparent overlay with artwork to complement base art.

PLATES: Plates are made photographically from your paste-up. The printer puts plates on the press to print your product. The printer will include a plate-making charge in your bill. If you think you will print your project again, ask for the plates.

PASTE-UP: The paste-up is what you produce with all your drawings, lettering, clip art, and rubber cement. You take your camera-ready paste-up to the printer.

REDUCTION/ENLARGEMENT: Changing the size of a piece of art. Reductions and enlargements are usually expressed in percentages. A 66 percent reduction will give you a finished product that is approximately two-thirds the size of the original.

 plus 66 percent reduction equals

You can buy a device known as a "reduction wheel" which will help you easily and accurately calculate percentages of enlargements and reductions.

REVERSE OR REVERSE OUT: Making a negative image—something a printer can do for you. This is the easy way to put white letters on a black or colored background.

Draw your letters like this:  Reverse them out like this:

SCREEN: The process by which a continuous tone photo is broken into tiny black dots so that the printing press can print it. Dots vary in size. The eye sees the dots as varying shades of gray, the larger dots appearing darker. The number of dots in an inch is called the line number. The more dots in an inch, the better the printed photo will appear. High quality printing jobs have 250 or more lines in an inch. Low quality printing jobs (like newspaper photos) have less than 100 lines in an inch. A small print shop can usually deliver about 150 line screens.

SCREEN DOTS: A large sheet of adhesive-backed plastic film on which dots have been printed. Screen dots come in various lines to an inch (see "SCREEN" above). When stuck to a piece of art and trimmed, the dots look gray. Use screen dots to add perspective and depth to your clip art. Avoid extremely fine dots because they may drop out when printed on a small press or photocopier. Dots and many other patterns are available at good art supply stores.

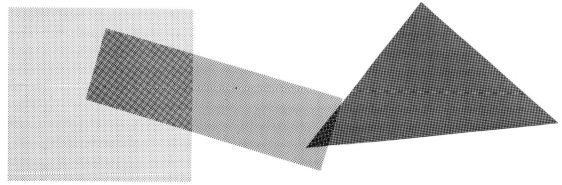

DO NOT try to screen your continuous tone photographs with screen dots. It doesn't work.

STAT: A high quality photographic reproduction of any art work. If you want to place two exact images side by side on your paste-up, have your printer make a stat of the original art. Rubber cement the stat down next to the original.

Original

plus stat equals

TRANSFER OR RUB-ON LETTERS: You may purchase pre-printed letters that you transfer onto your artwork. A large variety of rub-on and peel-and-stick letters is available at your art supply store. Look through the manufacturers' catalogs for ideas.

TYPO (TYPOGRAPHICAL ERROR): One of these days, it's going to happen! No matter how many times you proofread your finished paste-up, when you take delivery of your printed product the first thing you'll see will be an outrageously obvious mistake.

AND SO . . .

A piece of camera-ready art can contain many elements: drawings, screened photos, screen dots, an overlay or two, stats that have been flopped or reversed out, headlines and body copy, rub-on letters, etc., etc., etc. But don't worry! Take one step at a time, and you can produce appealing printed pieces for your Sunday School.

Just a reminder: When it comes to printed pieces, especially when you're just getting started, keep it simple. We hope we have helped you do just that.

TIPS ON PHOTOCOPYING

If the print shop is too far away, or if you don't need the high quality a printing press offers, or if you have only a few dozen copies to make, then you will want to run your job on a photocopy machine. Here are a few tips to keep in mind.

- Be careful to eliminate all possible sources of shadows on your paste-up sheet. Shadows are caused by the edges of artwork you've glued to the paste-up. See the sketch for examples of where shadows are likely to form.

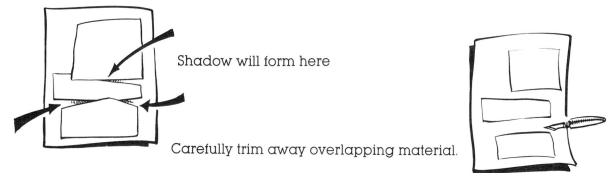

Shadow will form here

Carefully trim away overlapping material.

You can prevent shadows by avoiding sharp edges and by flooding correction fluid around the offending areas. Or you can make a photocopy and cover all shadows with correction fluid especially made for use on copies. Then use your corrected copy to make additional copies. Also, try lightening the exposure control on the copy machine.

- If your church doesn't have an office copier, shop around by phone for the lowest priced photocopying services. (Look in the Yellow Pages under "Printers" and "Photo Copying.") A print shop usually offers the lowest price, but try the post office, the library, the stationery store and the chain drug stores.

- You may find that if you need more than a few dozen copies, it is cheaper to have your copies printed on a printing press.

- Plain paper copiers are versatile. They allow you to print on both sides of the page, on any color paper, and usually in more than one size or in odd sizes. Most plain paper copiers can also print on cardstock. Experiment.

- You can buy specially made overhead projector transparencies and run them through plain paper copiers. Be sure to use transparencies made to be used in photocopiers. If you use the wrong kind and the acetate jams in the machine, the transparency can melt inside the hot copier! (Yuck!)

- Cartridge copiers often print several different colors of ink. You can produce multi-colored handbills on cartridge copiers.

119